7 TR's THAT HELP MANAGE YOUR DESTINY

Tarupiwa Muzah

Copyright © 2017. All rights reserved.

No part of this publication may be reproduced, stored in a retrieval system or transmitted in any way by any means, electronic, mechanical, photocopy, recording or otherwise, without the prior permission of the author except as provided by USA copyright law.

The opinions expressed by the author are not necessarily those of Revival Waves of Glory Books & Publishing.

Published by Revival Waves of Glory Books & Publishing

PO Box 596 l Litchfield, Illinois 62056 USA

www.revivalwavesofgloryministries.com

Revival Waves of Glory Books & Publishing is committed to excellence in the publishing industry.

Book design Copyright © 2017 by Revival Waves of Glory Books & Publishing. All rights reserved.

Published in the United States of America

Paperback: 978-1-365-84431-7

Table of Contents

CHAPTER 1 TRUST - INVESTMENT/HOPE IN 4

CHAPTER 2 TRY - ACTION 8

CHAPTER 3 TRIM - CUT BACK/CUT COSTS 11

CHAPTER 4 TRADE - EXCHANGE IDEAS 14

CHAPTER 5 TREAT - IMPRESS/GIVE YOUR BEST 17

CHAPTER 6 TRAIN - HELP OTHERS/BE A LEADER 20

CHAPTER 7 TRIUMPH - BE SUCCESSFUL/WIN A VICTORY 23

CHAPTER 1
TRUST - INVESTMENT/HOPE IN

They say put your money where your mouth is meaning make an investment to the direction you desire. Don't just speak it; show that you value it by investing in it.

Destiny is all about trust. When you trust, you hope in. What you hope in, you give your all, and you give your time and energy.

So firstly, you must find out where your mouth is for you to make an investment that will give you a maximum return. You can't invest in something that you don't love. If you do that type of a deal, you will lose out because you lack that drive to push that type of business.

Your passion can move you to your destiny. Discover what you are made of, what gets you going and what you do easily with a lot of joy in it.

What is it you love? What's in your heart is what you must focus on. In God we trust written on the cash is a show of focus and direction. To trust is to depend on, to give your all hoping for a great return.

It's better to trust in God than to trust in man who has no help for you. First things first. Before you look for a job that you will be given by man, look for God who owns the earth and all its fullness. You will see the difference as he will give you the revelation of your true purpose and your gift. After that, you will know exactly where to go.

You are a man of great inventions but you will not invent anything when you have a wrong focus. A wrong focus is a wrong trust. It's a bad investment to trust in people sometimes because they will turn you down. They promise you something and they never fulfill it. If you work for people, you will be disappointed but if you work as unto God, you are the happiest being.

Give your time and space to God, your Father, you will discover your true self and you will enter your destiny. Hope in him, and he won't let you down. Man will go away from you but not God; he will be the closest and be there in the times of need.

Jeremiah 17 verse 5-8 - Thus saith the Lord; cursed be the man that trusteth in man, and maketh flesh his arm, and whose heart departeth from the Lord. For he shall be like the heath in the desert, and shall not see when good cometh; but shall inhabit the parched places in the wilderness, in a salt land and not inhabited.

Blessed is the man that trusteth in the Lord, in whose hope the Lord is. For he shall be as a tree planted by the waters, and that spreadeth out her roots by the river, and shall not see when heat cometh, but her leaf shall be green; and shall not be careful in the year of drought, neither shall cease from yielding fruit.

If you involve God in your search for true meaning, you are blessed. If you focus on God as the foundation to your success, that's a strong foundation; he will surely sustain you and your building will never fall.

The man made things won't last, only the word of the Lord will live forever. Get the word as you depend on God which will be an eternal blessing, which will guarantee your victory and breakthrough in the coming future.

If you invest in the systems of this world, as they crumble you will also fall with them but if you invest in the things of God, your blessing is sure and it will last. So the best is to find him, find his will for your life and you will make it.

Involve the Holy Spirit as your guide and he will lead you to all the truth concerning your destiny. Revelation will come to you; you will see what eye has never seen before. You will become great.

So you must know where to put your money, your energy, your time and your resources firstly before you do anything else. Lay a good foundation for the future as you invest in God.

Mathew 6 verses 19-21 - Lay not up for yourselves treasures upon earth, where moth and rust doth corrupt, and where thieves break through and steal. But lay up for yourselves treasures in heaven, where neither moth nor rust doth corrupt, and where thieves do not break through nor steal. For where your treasure is, there will your heart be also.

Choose whom you shall serve, money or God, you can't serve two masters. Seek first the Kingdom of God and his righteousness, and all these other things will be added to you.

Those who hope in their treasures ,they accumulate and store them somewhere, and those who hope in God, we see them by their actions, they give out to his work.

Your search shows your desire; your desire shows your destiny. To really manage well the issue of your destiny, search for God, you will find him; you will know the true you, your product, your idea, and your gift. Let your will be God's will and your dream be God's dream.

Invest in God and you will know what he has invested in you; you will discover your true value then you will command your value as you go out there to make a difference.

Psalm 52 verses 7-8 - Lo, this is the man that made not God his strength; but trusted in the abundance of his riches, and strengthened himself in his wickedness. But I am like a green olive tree in the house of God; I trust in the mercy of God forever and ever. I praise God because he has done it.

CHAPTER 2
TRY - ACTION

Yes, trusting in God has made you to discover what you have; now you have to give it out. You have to put action to your discovery. Experiment with your gift and your skills and you will see things happen.

They call it trial and error meaning you can make mistakes but don't fear because you are getting developed in the process. The only failure is failure to try. Give it a try and you run away from those ones who just talk it and not do it.

The doing part takes a lot of courage and passion; it is the differentiating factor between men and boys. Boys speak and keep speaking, men do and keep doing. As you do, you will grow in knowledge and understanding of your craft.

Until action is put to your dream, it is a mere wish. Just to dream only without going for it, it's a waste of energy. You are free to try; nobody is holding you back, but yourself.

Ecclesiastes 5 verse 12 - The sleep of a laboring man is sweet...

You feel good when you try. You will only be satisfied after you have put effort to use your skills for the help of others. Do something with your gift and you will rest well when you sleep. Peace comes after action. You know that you have done something and that thing is a seed to a future of impact and destiny.

Be an industrious somebody who just goes on to try things, try to do business and you will be blessed through that attitude. Being active will not let you down.

The biggest enemy to your destiny is laziness; you can easily see that you have it by your unfinished projects. It can also be seen on those who talk too much and have nothing to show for their talk.

Ecclesiastes 9 verse 10 - Whatsoever thy hand findeth to do, do it with thy might; for there is no work, nor device, nor knowledge, nor wisdom, in the grave, wither thou goest.

Use your time wisely because you might never know when you will be leaving this body of yours. Take your chance on life and go for it and you will discover your greatness.

If you find something to do, don't wait too much for a season to start doing it. Jump into that opportunity of the day given to you. Make something of each day and you will soon be an expert of execution.

Use all your strength in the project at hand and be a person of excellence. Be available and useful; aim for the impossible and do what you can. Soon limitations will break down in front of you and you will go to heights that you never dreamt possible.

The best time to start is now. Speak against relaxing and sleep; look at it as an enemy and it will soon run away from you. You will surely enter your destiny as you work hard and do more. Try and try and try again. More gain comes from a little more pain. Take a step to your future and move to your destiny.

CHAPTER 3
TRIM - CUT BACK/CUT COSTS

You must cut the unnecessary away from your schedule and reduce wastage. Don't waste your dollars and time on mundane issues; Issues that have nothing to do with your destiny. Take those things and put them far from your visibility and you will benefit.

Take off the extra weight and the baggage; reduce it by trimming your tasks and making sure you are only doing things about your gifting and about those skills that help in your destiny exploits.

It's about priorities; you must set them in order putting first those things that give you the best value. What is it that you can be the best in the whole world at? Look at yourself, your gifts and talents. Find that thing and devote all your dollars and time to it.

All the other things you are spending your money and time doing that you feel they are less valuable, cut them away from you.

They are costly to you; those are unnecessary expenses so cut back and reduce those costs. You will be much more profitable when you stick to one and master that one until it grows to the level of excellence.

If you are in business, you need to cut back on your spending budget for you to realize greater profits. You must gather information on how day to day tasks are being handled, look for those things that are taking too much money but not bringing in the return and stop doing them. Things like unnecessary phone bills, employees using phones for personal issues.

Cutting back on something can be a painful experience for some but it will surely bring back good results as you follow through that type of objective.

John 15 verses 2-3 - Every branch in me that beareth not fruit he taketh away; and every branch that beareth fruit, he prunes it, that it may bring forth more fruit.

The pruning process is when God cuts back on the useless things in your life that are hindering your progress so that you will be much more profitable. Allow him to do that in you and you will be effective and enter your destiny.

Cut back every weight that slows you and run the race without attachment to the things of the world. Be clear on what you do and what you must stop doing to progress in life.

Hebrews 12 verse 1 - Wherefore seeing we also are compassed about with so great a cloud of witnesses, let us lay aside every weight, and sin which doth so easily beset us, and let us run with patience the race that is set before us.

Lay aside sin, cut it back from you because it hinders your destiny; it will cost you a lot. Reduce that cost and you will be blessed and reach your destiny.

If you haven't given your life to Jesus, say, "Lord Jesus, come into my heart and be my Lord and savior, forgive me of my sins and make me a child of God, I believe you died and rose on the third day, and through your blood I'm cleansed, thank you Father, I'm a new creation now in the name of Jesus Christ, Amen."

If you prayed this prayer, you are now saved; you are now a blessed child of God. You have cut back on sin. It was a hindrance to you, now you are free to rise, stand and enter your destiny.

CHAPTER 4
TRADE - EXCHANGE IDEAS

Start a conversation and build a network, exchange ideas with others, then you will manage well the issue of your destiny. Don't be a person who says, "I take nothing from no one." You won't make it with that attitude.

Those people who make it are not those who start something completely new but those who take ideas from others and enhance them, enlarge them, advance them and make the most out of them.

Something completely new can be hard to handle because you have to invest many dollars to advertise to customers to make them familiar with it.

So go on and make a trade. In a conversation, you trade information because you give some and take some. Look for opportunities to share ideas and get inspired by others in the same line of work or gifting you are pursuing. Exposure is the catalyst to a great destiny.

There are platforms of exchange; use them and follow through, have someone you look up to and get a lot of motivation from that individual. Give a complement then others will open up to you and will give you tips on how to get to another level of impact in the things you are doing.

Be part of a social network, volunteer and be in a club or group of people making a difference and soon you will learn new things and be better in your endeavors. As you share on what you know, others will help you also.

Proverbs 18 verse 24 - A man that has friends must show himself friendly; and there is a friend that sticketh closer than a brother.

Communication skills are essential in the management of your destiny exploits. You must develop that skill to relate well with others. You gain access to others when you sow into them. Be thankful for the little things others do for you and soon they will shower you with ideas that will catapult you to the next level.

Someone once said, "A friend in need is a friend indeed." You must be in need of others help and you also must be willing to help them when they need you. Then exchange has value to both sides.

One good idea can change your destiny. Gather ideas from different sources; look at them carefully and take the best one and use it wisely.

You are one idea away from your next big break so you must get into the habit of reading books, exchange tapes and material with other people and you will make it and manage well.

You say you are in a situation but know right now that they are countless ideas out there that are designed to solve that issue. All you have to do is be willing to make an exchange. Be willing to go for the trade and you will see the difference.

Cherish your connections and your connections will cherish you. Love others and they will give back that love to you. Get ideas from others and soar to greater heights.

CHAPTER 5
TREAT - IMPRESS/GIVE YOUR BEST

Everybody loves quality things. Every girl loves a boy who takes good care of himself, who has a clean shave and dresses nicely. They say elegance is an attitude.

The things you do must be of high quality standards and by doing it that way; you will not miss your destiny. Quality should be the biggest objective in your company.

Let people see where you are going by the way you dress. Your dress shows your expectation. If you are expecting success, you must dress as if you are already in it. Create a wow moment in everything you do. Give your best and do it to the best of your ability.

Inspiration is evident where there is fascination. Let others be fascinated by the way you handle things. Set the pace in quality and everyone will love to be associated with you. If you give out a sub-standard product, you are not cheating people, you are cheating yourself. Word of mouth will soon catch up on you. People will motivate others to disengage from your services and you will lose out.

Ecclesiastes 10 verse 3 - Yea, also, when he that is a fool walketh by the way, his wisdom faileth him, and he saith to everyone that he is a fool.

People can see your wisdom by the way you handle yourself. A fool does things in a haphazard way and does not care about the details. Everyone can easily see that disorder and it hinders in your destiny pursuit.

To manage your destiny well, you must always care about the details and seek to impress your customers. Give them what they can't find anywhere and you will be their only source of satisfaction. Never try to earn and gain without any effort in giving to the best of your ability.

What people perceive to be the best of quality is what you must discover and then implement that and you will soon gain their attention. Treat others in an excellent way and that experience will not be erased from their memory. They will remember you when you least expect it.

Quality brings comfort and everybody wants to dwell with comfortable things. It comes from material and a lot of concentration. Be principled in the way you do your things, make sure you replace the old machinery with the new. Be wise and stand for the cutting edge, the top of the line service that cannot be compared with any other.

1 Kings 10 verses 4-5 - And when the queen of Sheba had seen all Solomon's wisdom, and the house that he had built. And the meat of his table, and the sitting of his servants, and the attendance of his ministers, and their apparel, and his cupbearers, and his ascent by which he went up unto the house of the Lord; there was no more spirit in her.

People love to associate with prosperity and success so the way you handle your gift, your skill or business should show a sign of prosperity and you will gain ground.

CHAPTER 6
TRAIN - HELP OTHERS/BE A LEADER

To be an effective leader, first you have to lead yourself. Make sure that you achieve more, and what you do works and then people will love to follow. When they want to be involved, you must be willing to train them and show them the way it's done.

You must teach through video or demonstration so that others know the way to do it and be effective. The teaching tools may differ but you must just make sure you are progressing; people understand what it's all about.

You must define your mission in a clear way to those who want to follow you. Help them see what you see so that they run with you to the desired goal.

You can also train others by observation. You must know that people are looking at you; they are seeing all your moves so to help them effectively, just set an example by your everyday schedule. Impartation comes by observing. When others see you working hard and doing things on time, they easily copy that behavior.

When you are an honest individual, you can discover that those who surround you also become honest in the way they handle things.

We can look at David in the cave of Adulum, those men who came to him were weak man and in debt but see what happened. Their association with a mighty man of war, David, made them to become warriors and afterwards they did more exploits than him.

When you train others, you multiply yourself; you won't remain one. That becomes a sign that you are a true leader. More work is done and production increases when others are involved in what you do.

2 Timothy 2 verse 2 - And the things that thou hast heard of me among many witnesses, the same commit thou to faithful men, who shall be able to teach others also.

A true leader is not jealous of others abilities but is the one willing to nurture them. Help bring others to their full potential and you are a candidate for great leadership. You should not withhold information but give it out to the benefit of others. Be a giver as a leader, sow into others and you will gain respect among them.

Look also to the things of others and you will see yourself being blessed. What you have is for others, be committed to help them and later they will also do the same for you.

Job 29 verse 11 - When the ear heard me, then it blessed me; and when the eye saw me, it gave witness to me because I delivered the poor that cried, and the fatherless, and him that had none to help him. The blessing of him that was ready to perish came upon me; and I caused the widow's heart to sing for joy.

It's only when Job prayed for his friends that he received double for his trouble, so go ahead and help others and you will see the difference.

The best way to learn is to teach others and the best way to earn is to bless others. The blessing will come back to you, a good measure.

CHAPTER 7
TRIUMPH - BE SUCCESSFUL/WIN A VICTORY

It's only the grace of God that makes one come to this stage of winning a victory. You have achieved your goal, now you celebrate and rejoice.

Achievement takes a lot of effort and concentration. When you are successful in one thing, you will become an influence to people in many other things. You will be an effective leader. People will listen to the words you say.

You are now a comfort and a source of inspiration to many. Success is how you succeed successfully; only you can best define your own success. When you play according to your strength and you push yourself to the limit, then you will come to the stage of triumph.

You are born to triumph! You are not a mistake and God has wired you for success. He has put the Holy Spirit inside of you so that you can't fail. He has designed you to pass and he is the one who leads you to that victory.

2 Corinthians 2 verse 14 - Now thanks be unto God, which always causeth us to triumph in Christ, and maketh manifest the savour of his knowledge by us in every place.

So you must be thankful to the creator God, because with him you have become an achiever. You see and meet victory at every step. You are empowered to make a difference and to become great. When you are in line with your purpose and gift, you are a champion and you succeed in every move you make.

Even your preparation was unique. God knew exactly what's needed for your success and destiny. This is how he causes you to triumph; he prepares you and then gives you opportunities to be of impact. He revealed to you your hidden abilities, now you shine as light and you shine so bright.

He has put valuable things inside of you so the time has come for that value to manifest to all and now you are strengthened to fulfill you call.

In the beginning God, so as you began with God, you come to the victory. You were willing to follow the real order of life which is involving God in the details of your being. Now you reap the benefits of such an attitude.

Hebrews 13 verses 20-21 - Now the God of peace, that brought again from the dead our Lord Jesus, that great shepherd of the sheep, through the blood of the everlasting covenant, make you perfect in every good work to do his will, working in you what is pleasing in his sight, through Jesus Christ; to whom be glory forever and ever. Amen.

Our God is a faithful God; the one who made his son Jesus to be victorious and to rise again from the grave. He has perfected you in your gifting and talents, and has made you to rise from obscurity to impact. He has helped you to manage well the issue of your destiny. To him be the Glory.

www.ingramcontent.com/pod-product-compliance
Lightning Source LLC
LaVergne TN
LVHW021749060526
838200LV00052B/3555